Healing Through Play – Using the Oaklander Model

A Guidebook for Therapists and Counselors Working with Children, Adolescents and Families

By

Karen Fried, PsyD, LMFT
Christine McKenna, LMFT, LPCC

Book Concept Designer
Shelley Short, BA S

Copyright© 2020 by Karen Fried, Christine McKenna and Shelley Short.

All rights reserved. No part of this book may be reproduced or used in any manner without written permission of the copyright owner except for the use of quotations in a book review.

First paperback edition June 2020

Book design by Shelley Short
Cover design by IsaDesignNet

Printed in the USA

ISBN: 9798218910129

This book is dedicated to Violet Oaklander who has inspired all of us to produce this guidebook so that her work continues to inspire and guide therapists, counselors and teachers worldwide.

We are so grateful to you for your work.

Acknowledgements

Kathy Miu, SM, is a business and technology consultant for companies ranging from Silicon Valley startups to the Fortune 500. She loves to pair her creative pursuits with her engineering background. Karen, Chris and Shelley want to wholeheartedly thank you for guiding us in the marketing, advertising and technology aspects of this project from the beginning until the end. Thank you for your keen intelligence, expertise and guidance. We couldn't have done this without you.

Alisa Reich, LMFT, PhD is a Licensed Marriage and Family Therapist and holds a PhD in history of medicine from UCLA. She is an experienced editor in the fields of neurophysiology, psychology, public administration, history, education, legal theory, drama, fiction, and liturgy. Thank you, Alisa, for being our wise and detail-minded editor. We appreciate the patience, perfectionism, experience and editing skills you brought to this project. You took our drafts and polished them to perfection.

Anthony Latagliata is a senior graphic designer with over 15 years of experience in the creative industry. He has worked with clients from community non-profits, to healthcare marketing initiatives and international dietary supplement distribution, and continues to do so with great passion. We are very grateful to you Tony for taking our drafts, and with expertise, working quickly and diligently to transform them into a layout for publication. Thank you very much.

VSOF Foundation Board and Friends of the Board

Peter Mortola, PhD, a founding board member of VSOF, is a Professor of Counseling Psychology and Coordinator of the School Psychology Program at Lewis and Clark College in Portland, Oregon. Peter, your book, *Windowframes*, was invaluable to us as we wrote our Guidebook. Many thanks for allowing us to use your conceptual graphics, and respectfully documenting Violet's own words so they can be used when introducing the exercises.

Christiane Elsbree, LCSW, founding member of VSOF, is a psychotherapist in private practice in Seattle, Washington. Thank you, Christiane for your positive, kind and truly expert contributions to VSOF.

Claire Mercurio, PhD, is a Psychologist who works with children, adolescents and adults in Santa Barbara, California. She is a founding member and Treasurer of VSOF. Thank you, Claire, for your dedicated service to VSOF. Your efforts allow us to manage the budget, which includes distribution of the scholarship fund that enables deserving therapists to attend training in the Oaklander Model.

Martha Oaklander and **Mha Atma Khalsa**, DC, are Violet's daughter-in-law and son who are tireless and unwavering supporters of VSOF. Thanks to your work on behalf of the foundation, Violet's work can be continued and shared.

Lynn Stadler, LMFT, is a Gestalt psychotherapist who works in private practice in Santa Barbara, California, a founding board member of the Violet Solomon Oaklander Foundation, and a co-founder of the Oaklander training program. Lynn you have done so much to further Violet's model in the US and internationally and we have all benefited. Thank you, Lynn, for your work on behalf of VSOF, as well as your partnership in using the Oaklander Model.

Sue Talley, LMFT, is a founding member and past President of VSOF, a co-founder of Oaklander training, and a psychotherapist in private practice in Agoura Hills, California. We are grateful to you Sue for your vision and leadership in founding VSOF, as well as your collaboration in training other therapists in the Oaklander Model.

Patric White, PhD, founding member of VSOF, specializes in child, adolescent and family therapy in Hermosa Beach, California. Thank you Patric for your wonderful work on behalf of VSOF.

Camille Jarmie Harris, PhD, is an integral member of VSOF, supporting us in organizing our conferences and currently managing the continuing education aspect of the Just for Now calls. We appreciate all you do Camille.

Most of the children I have seen for therapy have had two main difficulties: one, they do not make good contact (with books, teachers, other children, etc.) and two, they do not feel good about themselves (low self-concept). As therapists, it is not our job to "fix" them, but to help make them have better contact in their worlds and to feel better about themselves. Good contact involves learning to be present and to enhance contact functions; the senses, use of the body, understanding and expressing emotions and good use of the intellect.

As therapists, we use many projective and expressive techniques as well as specific experiences to achieve these goals.

Dr. Karen Fried and her colleagues have created a wonderful guidebook that gives many suggestions that can be used in the therapist's office. Therapists assess the child's needs and use techniques that are valuable, effective and useful. Besides all that, they are fun.

This book is truly a treasure.

Violet Oaklander

Table of Contents

3	Introduction
4	Key Concepts and Definitions
10	First Sessions
12	The Therapeutic Process
20	House Tree Person Drawing
22	Childhood Drawing
26	Safe Place Drawing
30	Rosebush Drawing
35	Emotions and Aggressive Energy
40	Anger Drawing
44	Clay Work
48	Grief
52	Grief Drawing
54	Brief Therapy
56	Polarities
58	Puppets
62	Picture Cards
64	Sand Tray Work
68	Self Nurturing / Self Acceptance
72	Demon Drawing
76	Music Process
80	Termination
83	Supplemental Activities
92	References
93	Appendix
103	Index

Visit us at
OaklanderTraining.org

| Workshops & Continuing Education | Virtual Play Therapy Tools |

| Demo Videos for the Oaklander Model | Supervision & Consultation |

Dear Reader,

Thank you for your interest in our *Healing Through Play Guidebook*. It is our aim to support you in promoting the well-being of children of any age in your care using this developmentally appropriate and fun approach. These young people might have been given all sorts of diagnoses—sensory processing disorder, anxiety, depression, learning problems, ADHD—but the philosophy guiding our guidebook applies to all: **No matter what the diagnosis, a child is still a child.**

So we encourage you to connect with the whole child, and not get stuck defining them in terms of a diagnosis or problem. No matter what specific behaviors we see, we must not forget what this child, and all children really need: acceptance of who they are, love, and feeling heard. We must remember that when these needs are unfulfilled, youngsters may attempt to get them met through maladaptive behaviors difficult for others to tolerate.

The theory, interventions and activities presented here give you engaging and developmentally sensitive tools to help the children and adolescents in your care express those essential needs and get them met in healthy ways. And while you may adjust your vocabulary to match the knowledge and experience of your clients, you will find that the interventions themselves stretch to accommodate not just their developmental stage but their individual uniqueness.

Sincerely,

Karen Fried

Christine McKenna

Introduction

We created this guidebook to serve as a companion to the **Oaklander Training Program** Violet developed after publishing *Windows to Our Children*. Child and adolescent therapists came from all over the world to attend her life-changing two-week intensive workshops in Santa Barbara, California. This training continues in Santa Monica, California (led by Karen Fried) and in other places in the United States and international venues by facilitators whom Violet trained, including Lynn Stadler and Peter Mortola.

While this guidebook is meant to be used by therapists who have participated in Violet's training process, that experience is not a requirement. Here, we outline Violet's thinking as well as some of her classic experiential exercises for you to use when a child or adolescent comes to therapy. Introduction to the model includes how to conduct a first session and how to take developmental factors into account. The guide then explains key elements of Violet's signature focus on a young client's ability to contact (inwardly and outwardly), and details how you can enable youngsters at any developmental stage to develop healthy contact functions and to strengthen their sense of self.

In addition, this guidebook outlines Violet's approach to the emotions-including the universal but often-misunderstood ones of anger and aggressive energy that can be challenging to handle in a therapy session. To support you in doing so, the guidebook leads you, step by step, through many of her most effective projective techniques, such as the Safe Place and Rosebush drawings and working with clay, sand tray, and puppets. Finally, it lays out the self-nurturing process, often arising at the end of therapy, and explicates Violet's insights on developmental issues impacting termination for you to apply in your own practice. Thus we present Violet's work and, with her blessing, have endeavored to make it even more accessible to therapists. Whether we cite her words verbatim or not, Violet's knowledge, wisdom, and deep love of young people inspires every line.

We hope you enjoy using this guidebook as much as we have enjoyed composing it.

Key Concepts and Definitions:

What is Gestalt therapy with children?

Before we define the term, know that it's not necessary to be a Gestalt Therapist to use this guidebook. But Violet Oaklander found the model of Gestalt Therapy ideal for helping children and adolescents. *Gestalt* is the German word for "whole," and Gestalt Therapy focuses on the whole person and on revealing and integrating all aspects of that person's physical, emotional, and intellectual self. Below are a few central Gestalt concepts Violet employed so successfully with youngsters.

1. The I / Thou relationship

The Oaklander Model builds on philosopher Martin Buber's core value: the I-Thou relationship (1958). Violet understood that establishing what Buber considered an authentic relationship—honest, direct, specific to the individuals—is the essential foundation for any therapy. Nothing happens without it, and it needs to be nurtured. As Violet observed, the I-Thou relationship has specific aspects that are especially important in work with children at any age. Buber taught that, for an authentic connection, we must meet each other as two separate individuals, neither superior to the other. This means that when interacting with even the youngest child, the authentic therapist does not judge or make assumptions about the child, but accepts her or his current and real self. The therapist must be present and in relationship with the child. In this way the relationship will be nurtured. In therapy, the therapist gives children the opportunity to experience and strengthen their unique sense of self, and thus improve their relational skills with others. In the same way, the therapist's adhering to her or his own boundaries creates a safe, self-respectful and authentic space for the child or adolescent.

2. Contact and Resistance

Being in *contact* means a person is fully present with all aspects of the self—physical senses, emotional awareness and expression, and intellect—and thereby with others and the environment. Healthy infants are born with a capacity to be in contact with their environment. But children of any age who experience difficulties may cut themselves off from their awareness of one or more of these crucial elements of their self. Restricting or burying awareness of one or some of these parts of the self compromises the growth of the child's healthy sense of self. Interestingly, one sign of good contact is the ability to withdraw from a person or a situation that is not in one's best interest. So children without contact skills may be both distanced from aspects of their inner self and stuck in problematic relationships or positions.

Resistance in a child or adolescent is a natural defense against experiencing something when they don't feel supported. On the flip side, if a youngster shows no resistance, Violet says, "this can be a sign that their sense of self is so fragile that she must do whatever she is told to do in order to feel that she can survive." Therapists (and all adults) need to keep in mind that a young person's resistance is a highly functional protective armor which deserves to be heeded and honored. It hides—in fact, guards—important material they need to work through, but cannot as yet. When their resistance is acknowledged and respected, children may be willing to risk "trying on" a new behavior and letting the old maladaptive one drop away.

3. Awareness and Experience

Oaklander's therapeutic process allows children of all ages to strengthen their sense of self by becoming aware of—becoming in contact with—their own process, sensations, feelings, needs, wants, thinking, and actions.

4. The Senses and the Body

Interventions involving the physical aspect of the whole child allow them to develop contact with their five senses as well as to experience sensations in their bodies. Examples include:

Touch: finger painting, using clay, sand tray

Sight: looking at pictures, kaleidoscopes

Hearing: painting while listening to music; using musical instruments

Taste: tasting segments of an orange and comparing that taste with the therapist's description; talking about favorite tastes and not-so-favorite tastes

Smell: experience different scents of flowers, fruit, grass.

The Body: fun activities in the session aim to heighten youngsters' awareness of their bodies. Games such as charades, Simon Says, and puppet shows, as well as attending to their breath as a hint about their internal states, are all helpful.

5. Sense of Self

Children with a clear sense of self have an awareness of their body, emotions, and intellect. Healthy young people constantly express who they are and who they are not, either directly or indirectly.

6. Contact / Boundary Disturbances

Ideally, children perceive contact between parts of themselves and between themselves and others. Disturbances occur when they experience harm from the environment. Since they are not yet capable of setting their own boundaries, harmful external contact causes internal disturbance, which diminishes their sense of self.

7. Self- Regulation

Children of any age seek emotional *homeostasis*—constant re-balancing—in response to upsetting events. A healthy sense of self aids their self-regulation to life's minor challenges. But when under unmanageable stress, they may resort to maladaptive behaviors, such as acting out or withdrawing, to get their need for calming regulation met.

8. Emotions

Self-support is a prerequisite for the expression of blocked emotions. Emotional expression work lets children find and support their true self by helping them understand what feelings are, come to know their own feelings, express feelings whose earlier blocking interfered with healthy functioning, and learn skills to articulate risky feelings like anger in safe, healthy ways. A variety of creative, expressive and projective modalities facilitates this work: drawing, clay, puppets, sand tray scenes, storytelling, music and play-acting.

9. Introjection, Confluence, Deflection and Retroflection

Introjection
Children, especially the youngest, lack the maturity and cognitive capacity to reject characterizations of themselves which don't fit. Thus they may easily *introject*, or take in, negative or inaccurate messages and develop a faulty belief system about their self.

Confluence
Confluence means merging—the antithesis of the individuation supported by a strong sense of self. Confluent behavior is common among youngsters who have difficulty establishing their boundaries.

Deflection

Children, including adolescents, use *deflection*—shifting away the focus—to avoid dealing directly with material and emotions they find too difficult or painful.

Retroflection

Children of any age may engage in *retroflection*—displacement onto themselves—when they can't deal directly with an issue. They may retroflect the emotion of grief by turning it inward, and endure physical symptoms such as stomachaches or headaches.

10. Self-Nurturing Work

The focus of *self-nurturing work* is to help the child reframe negative messages about the self which she or he introjected at an earlier age. Revealing those negative views—now, parts—of the self, and learning to respect and nurture them, make this work especially powerful.

11. Polarities

Children and adolescents benefit from gaining an experience and awareness of the polarities that exist within them. They may be overly aware of one part, like their "bad" qualities, and the therapist can provide them with an awareness of the polarity, i.e.; what's "good," about them. Please see the exercise to work with this concept on page 57.

12. Unfinished Business

Past trauma that has not been dealt with—*unfinished business*—can result in current maladaptive behavior. Part of the Oaklander therapeutic process involves identifying and addressing these unresolved issues.

What Brings Children to Therapy

In Violet's view, children, including adolescents, are brought into therapy for two reasons:

Difficulty making good contact with one or more contact functions; intellect, senses, body, and emotions.

A poor sense of self. Children who have a poor sense of self often manifest signs of being blocked from their emotions, have a hard time making choices for themselves and finding support in their environment when needed.

Educating parents about the process is essential.

I don't "fix" kids...

In the first session, according to this model, you, as the therapist clarify your role. Tell the parents:

While I don't "fix" kids, I do :

1. Help them feel better about themselves.
2. Help them feel happier, healthier, more peaceful and in better contact with their environment.
3. Help them express deep feelings - particularly anger in appropriate ways.
4. Help them experience blocked emotions.
5. Help parents set clear limits.

When a parent brings a child into therapy, it is usually because a parent and/or school wants something that has been problematic about the child's behavior to be "fixed." Violet's response, "I need to tell you that I don't fix kids. But let me tell what I do."

First Session | Issues & Considerations

1. **Meet with parents and children of any age together** so there are no secrets kept.
2. **Evaluate contact** between you and the client and between you and the parents. Begin setting up the I-Thou relationship, and mirror the client's level of activity or calm.
3. **Ask the client,** "Do you know why you're here?"
4. **POV** Get each person's point of view.
5. **Set boundaries** of time, fee, safety and office rules, ethical and legal considerations.
6. **Evaluate communication skills** of family.
7. **Gather information from the client first**
8. **Explain Procedure:**
   A. See client 3 to 5 times.
   B. Parents come back to "discuss what we'll do," opening possibility of varied configurations of therapy and other interventions.
   C. Give a brief explanation of therapy process.
9. **Establish responsibility** for coming to sessions.
10. **Discuss business procedures**
11. **Explain confidentiality** and importance of "no secrets."
12. **Ask the child or adolescent, "What do you want?"** (may differ from resolving the presenting problem)
13. If there's time, bring up issue of **anger** and ask how it is expressed in the family.
14. **Ask how discipline is handled in the family.**

Developmental Factors

Developmental issues can affect how the child functions throughout life. In order to survive, cope, and get needs met, a child with a poorly matured sense of self may inhibit and anesthetize the senses, restrict the body, block emotions, close down the intellect, and adopt inappropriate ways of being in the world.

Confluence vs. Struggle for Self
A dilemma: The newborn gets their sense of self from the primary care giver—their voice, touch, face. Yet the growing child struggles against this merging in order to individuate.

Egocentricity
The child, especially in the earliest years, is cognitively and emotionally unable to understand external, separate experience. Thus the child blames the self for any trauma experienced.

Introjects
Lacking the maturity and cognitive capacity to reject or ignore hurtful or inaccurate descriptions of the self, the young child takes in negative or wrong characterizations and develops a faulty belief system about the self.

Getting Needs Met
Children will try anything to get basic needs for acceptance, love, and being heard met, and to avoid rejection and abandonment—including the inappropriate behaviors and the symptoms that bring them into therapy.

Expressing Emotions
Many children have learned early that expressing emotions, particularly anger, is unacceptable. This part of the therapeutic process allows for healthy ways to recognize and convey blocked emotions.

Limit Setting
For the health and safety of the young person, parents must set limits. But whether it's done lovingly or critically makes all the difference.

Cultural Expectations

Children quickly learn what is expected of them based upon the culture of the particular group in which they live. Conflicting messages and tensions can arise when they also grow up in a second, different culture.

Systems

Many systems besides the family affect a child's development, including schools, medical institutions, religious institutions, sports teams, and other social groups.

The Therapeutic Process

Establishing the Therapeutic Relationship

The young client and the therapist must spend time getting to know one another. This time allows them to build a sense of safety and trust and to set boundaries and limits. Without at least the start of an authentic, I-Thou relationship, nothing therapeutic can happen. If the therapist cannot establish a relationship, then that becomes the first and primary goal of the therapy.

Contact

Contact, we know, is the ability to be fully present internally and in interaction with another. When a youngster has difficulty staying in contact, the focus of the therapy is to strengthen their ability to sustain contact. The therapist must establish and evaluate contact at every session. At the same time resistance, a breaking of contact, must be recognized and honored as the client's way of coping with painful issues.

Contact Functions

The functions of contact include the awareness and use of the senses (touch, sight, hearing, smell, and taste), the body, emotional expression, and the intellect. Anxious or worried children and adolescents will restrict and inhibit these vital contact functions. Developing and enhancing these aspects of the whole person are primary goals in the therapeutic process.

Self-Support

Work in this area helps young people build inner strength through the expression of the self. As they begin to know and define themselves through identifying and expressing their wishes, needs, likes, dislikes, ideas and opinions, they gain the skill of self-support.

Providing the child of any age with experiences of making choices, of mastery, and of power—as many of Violet's engaging activities do—greatly facilitates the growth of that crucial self-support.

Emotional Expression

Self-support lays the foundation for expressing emotions. As noted, emotional expression work assists children at any stage in understanding emotions, recognizing their own, and learning ways to convey even tough ones, like anger, appropriately. For this, the model uses a variety of projective techniques including drawing, clay, puppets, sand tray scenes, storytelling, music, and creative dramatics.

Self-Nurturing Work

This work aims to help the youngster reframe untrue or negative messages about the self that had been introjected at a younger age. Identifying those false depictions of the self and substituting self-support for shame is the essence of this process.

Dealing With Process

Generally, inappropriate behaviors melt away when the therapist and young client do the work detailed above. So it can be disappointing to therapists and parents—and to children—when youngsters continue for some time to utilize ineffective coping mechanism in an attempt to get their needs met. That's when you and everyone need patience and confidence in the process. Through the therapy sessions, the young person discovers and experiments with different ways of being in the world and gains new, more appropriate and more effective tools for obtaining support from the environment. Work with children is not so much for the awareness but for the experience.

Closing Session

This session brings closure and an empowering sense of accomplishment. Thus it helps children and adolescents learn they can let go and move on to the next stage of their development into independent individuals. Of course, they can deal only with the feelings and issues that fit their current maturation level. They may reach a plateau in their progress and then, at a later time, evidence new symptoms or behaviors that indicate they are ready for further work. So for the developing young person, the closing session is not necessarily a true termination.

Family Work and Parent Education

These tasks form an essential part of the therapy and may take place periodically. To facilitate the youngster's therapeutic process outside your office, you may wish to ask family members to experiment with new behaviors.

The therapeutic process is not necessarily linear.

We often go back and forth in order to give the child experiences as the needs for them present themselves.

Violet Oaklander

NOTE:

In *Hidden Treasures*, Violet articulates her belief "that the child enters the world with full capacity for emotional health." The goal of the Oaklander model is to find a way to help the child express themself through play. The therapist strives to help the child feel happier in the world, develop a stronger sense of self, cope with stress, and find healthy and appropriate ways to deal with emotions. Symptoms and behaviors that are concerning to adults are an indication that a child is experiencing an interruption of this "capacity." The therapist's task is to support the child in their non-linear path to life and growth and to help them at any stage of that process.

The Oaklander Model

Sequence of Dr. Oaklander's Work

1. IMAGINATIVE EXPERIENCE
" Imagine it"

2. SENSORY EXPRESSION
" Make it"

3. NARRATIVE/METAPHORIC DESCRIPTION
" Be it"

4. SENSE-MAKING ARTICULATION
" Does it fit for you"

Adapted from
Peter Mortola, *Windowframes*
School of Counseling Psychology
Lewis and Clark College
pmortola@clark.edu

Using Projective Techniques

Gauge the client's readiness to use projective techniques. At each step throughout this process, **watch for resistance**: Observe the client's body language and other evidence of affect (stiffening, losing focus, deflective behaviors). If resistance emerges, respect it and move onto another activity, knowing you can revisit an issue when the client is ready.

But careful assessment is important—a confluent child or adolescent may agree with everything; one out of contact with the intellect (or too young) may not understand what you are asking; you may be off the mark; or the young client may not feel enough support to own anything. Watch for patterns, themes, polarities, and stuck places.

The Client's Therapeutic Steps:

1. **Willingness to do a projective activity** (drawing, clay, puppets, sand tray, storytelling).

2. **Telling about** what they produced to the therapist or someone else. Telling how it felt to do it or how they did it. Sharing the experience of doing it by talking about it.

3. **Entering into the metaphor,** or the image.
   -Becoming part of the picture—being the object, the puppet, or other characters, giving details.
   -Seeing the situation from the perspective of the object or as a part of the whole.
   -Able to answer, "Which one is you?" and "Describe yourself."
   -Dialoging with the object. Able to answer, "What's going on? What's happening?" and to tell the story.

4. **Owning the projection.** This can be done at two levels.
   A. Symbolic level: The young person can tell about the situation, but only as metaphor. That is, fragmentation between the internal and external meanings continues within the personality.
   B. Reality/Personal level: The child or adolescent realizes that what is experienced within the metaphor is also experienced by them in real life. Making this connection deepens the work and allows what has been out of awareness to come into awareness. Asking, "Do you feel that way?" can move the young person into this deeper level of work.

Example: Toy exercise

"Choose a toy [with adolescents, you may say, "an object;" pause for time to choose]. Look over your toy [or object]. Become the [fill in: tree, animal, boat, etc.]. What's it like to be you?"

Projection takes place as the youngster moves away from the object—from the sensory experience of touching, seeing, or smelling it—into language and, more and more, into a story narrative.

The next section offers sample scripts for some of Violet's favorite projective techniques; feel free to tweak them.

We are so grateful to Peter Mortola who recorded Violet's actual wording in introducing most of these exercises. Along with the worksheets that Violet created for the trainings, we use her original wording and materials in this guidebook.

Thanks to Peter's documentation, you as the reader have the opportunity to learn about and guide clients using these exercises in Violet's own voice.

Materials & Tools:

- Paper : Newsprint / Printer Paper / Drawing Pad
- Tools : Chalk / Pastels / Crayons / Colored Pencils
- Hard Surface : Drawing Boards / Paper Pad Backing / Table

House Tree Person Drawing

Explanation:

1. Helps you **get to know** the child or adolescent.
2. Begins to establish **an I-Thou relationship.**
3. Promotes **contact.**
4. Lets the young person **feel honored and listened to.**
5. Client's making statements about the self **builds a sense of self.**
6. **Improves youngster's contact skills:** The client has drawn a picture; you look at it; the client looks at it; you say things; the client listens; the client accepts or rejects your statements; you honor the client's decisions. Throughout this process, the young person feels safe enough to stay in contact.
7. Tells you about the **child's or adolescent's process:** fast, slow, insecure (erases a lot), perfectionistic, chaotic, sparse/minimal, colorful.

Prompt:

"I would like you to draw a house, a tree, and a person on one piece of paper. Here are three sizes of paper and markers, crayons, pastels, and colored pencils. Chose what you would like to use. Would you like to use the couch? The table? The floor? You can put anything you want in the picture as long as it also has a house, a tree, and a person. [When the client is finished, say:] This picture tells me something about you, but I am not always right, so I have to check it out with you….

I see here that you keep a lot of things to yourself. Does that fit for you?" [If yes, ask if you can write on the picture. You might write, "Keeps a lot of things to herself."]

[When complete, read everything back to the youngster. Ask him or her to sign and date the picture.]

Materials & Tools:
- Paper : Newsprint / Printer Paper / Drawing Pad
- Tools : Chalk / Pastels / Crayons / Colored Pencils
- Hard Surface : Drawing Boards / Paper Pad Backing / Table

Childhood Drawing

Explanation:

This drawing is used for therapists taking the Oaklander Training to help them be in touch with their childhood's. In order to be helpful to children, it is important for therapists to be able to connect with their own childhood. It can also be used for children of any age to go back into an earlier time of their childhood's.

Prompt:

"We're going to begin with an experience now. What I'd like you to do is just to get as comfortable as you can in the place where you are sitting. I'd like you to close your eyes. I like to start these experiences with a little relaxation exercise. I do the exact same exercise with all the kids that I work with. All ages. So just kind of go into yourself, see how you feel. Notice if you have any aches or pains anywhere. Just notice it. Notice how your arms are placed, and how your legs are placed. Know that you can move anytime. If you want to change your position, it's ok. Feel the pressure of the chair and the floor against your body. Wiggle your toes. Notice how you breathe. What I'd like you to do is take a deep breath. Hold it, then let it out [therapist inhales, then exhales]. Let's do it once more. Notice when you let your breath out, your shoulders generally drop. Try that again. Take a deep breath and then let it out [therapist inhales, then exhales].

I am going to make a sound. I'd like you to listen to the sound for as long as you can [ring the chime twice].

What I'd like you to do is to go back to a time in your childhood. Some memory of your childhood that suddenly pops into your head when I say that. It could be a happy memory, it could be a sad memory, it could be an angry memory, or a mixed memory. Go back to a time….Go way back….[To adolescents, suggest, "it could be during middle school or as a young teenager."] Pick a time. Pick a memory. You don't have to have this memory in great detail. It could be a vague memory. Go back to this memory and notice what's happening to you in that memory. Where are you? What surrounds you? Who is with you, if anyone? Maybe you're not with anyone.

And then notice how you feel in this particular memory. Get a sense of what it was like for you to be this child. I am going to ask you in a minute to draw this. Always remember, I don't have to understand your drawing. You can use colors, lines, scribbles…whatever. You can use color or no color. However you want to do it. You might want to draw the feelings in colors, lines, shapes. You might want to draw stick figures to make it easy. It doesn't have to be a wonderful drawing. I'm not grading you on the drawing; it is just for you to set down this memory. So when you are ready, you can open your eyes and, without talking, I'd like you to get a drawing board and a piece of paper. Take a handful of pastels or markers and put them in a bowl. You can stay in the room, you can go outside or out on the patio. You'll have about 10 minutes to do this drawing. So when you are ready, I'd like you to do that."

Materials & Tools:
- Paper : Newsprint / Printer Paper / Drawing Pad
- Tools : Chalk / Pastels / Crayons / Colored Pencils
- Hard Surface : Drawing Boards / Paper Pad Backing / Table

Safe Place Drawing

Explanation:

Many children begin therapy without a sense of safety either externally in their environments and/or within themselves. This drawing can be helpful to give them a feeling of safety, and an inner resource to be able to access and express blocked emotions in the therapy. Violet advises if a child is unable to imagine a safe place, to first imagine and draw an "unsafe" place in order to help them connect with this concept.

Prompt:

"I'd like you to get as comfortable as you can where you are, and get as relaxed as you can. Close your eyes. I don't know if I've said this, but I always close my eyes when I tell young people to close their eyes because usually they don't close their eyes, and yet if I don't close my eyes we are both sitting looking at each other! So I close my eyes, because, of course, they are either peeking or squinting, and if they see me with my eyes closed, they feel safer to close their eyes. How do I know that? Because I am peeking. But I am not going to peek at you. So just close your eyes and just go into yourself, see how you're feeling, see if you have any aches or pains anywhere. Just notice it. Notice how your arms are placed, and how your legs are placed. Know that you can move anytime you want to.

Listen to any sounds you hear outside of the room. Notice your breath. Again, let's take a deep breath, hold it, then let it go [therapist inhales, then exhales]. Notice when you let your breath go, your shoulders tend to fall. Let's do that again [therapist inhales, then exhales]. It's ok to let a sound out when you let your breath out… it just floats away through the ceiling magically, or out the door, to balloon-land…. I am going to make a sound with this small chime; listen to the sound as long as you can [ring the chime twice].

I want you to imagine that you can go to a safe place, whatever safe means for you. Now this place could be any place. I would like you to think of one right now. Make up a place. It doesn't have to be perfect. Just choose a safe place and go there, and look around, notice the colors, the light, and the shadows. Maybe there are some particular smells to your place. Allow yourself to touch various things in your place, to feel temperature and texture. Of course if you happen to be barefoot, have your feet do this too. Notice what you do in your safe place: Are you doing something or are you just sitting? And what I'm going to ask you to do soon is to draw this place. And I want to remind you that I don't have to understand your drawing, no one has to. It's your drawing. It can be any way that you want it to be. If you need to draw something that you don't know how to draw, it could just be a shape and you'll know what it is. It could be abstract, or it can be as concrete as you want it to be, it could be any way. It could be a mixture. You might have a feeling of the place around the colors, lines and shapes. Just draw it any way that you want to."

Materials & Tools:

- Paper : Newsprint / Printer Paper / Drawing Pad
- Tools : Chalk / Pastels / Crayons / Colored Pencils
- Hard Surface : Drawing Boards / Paper Pad Backing / Table

Rosebush Drawing

Explanation:

The Rose Bush drawing is a classic projective activity that children enjoy. Violet has written regarding the rationale of the Rose Bush drawing, "I find that the use of guided fantasy and imagery is a powerful tool for helping children express blocked feelings, wishes, needs, wants, thoughts in a safe non-intrusive way. It is often easier for the young person to respond to a metaphor for his or her life than the harsh reality. The use of fantasy provides a bridge to the child's inner life. The child then can look at it, examine it; and when ready, own it. This "owning" of the aspects of the metaphor that fit provides the child with self-support and strengthens the child's self."

Prompt:

"I'd like you to just get as relaxed as you can. And just go inside yourself and see how you're feeling in there… see how your head feels, and your shoulders feel and your arms, your stomach, chest, back…5 second pause…wiggle your toes, sometimes we forget that we go all the way down to our toes. Take a deep breath [She inhales], hold it…and then let it out … [She exhales]. Let's do that a couple more times … [20 second pause]. I'm going to make a sound and just listen to the sound as long as you can."

[Ring a chime three times]…

"I'd like you to imagine that you are a rose bush, or any flower bush that we will call a rosebush. You can be tall or short, full or scrawny. Do you have thorns? Flowers? I If so, what color are they? Do you have roots? If so, where are they? Where are you? You can be anywhere, on the moon, in the middle of the ocean, in a yard–anywhere. Are there other bushes or trees near you? Animals? birds? A fence? Who takes care of you?

Draw the rosebush and whatever else is in your mind's picture."

Table 1: Violet's Prompts for Metaphoric or Narrative Description

	Imaginary Experience **IMAGINE IT**	Sensory Experience **MAKE IT**	Metaphoric Narrative Articulation **BE IT**	Sense Making Application **DOES THIS FIT?**
House Tree Person Drawing	"I'd like you to draw a house, a tree, and a person on one piece of paper."	Draws with pastels / crayons / colored pencils	"This house with only a few windows tells me that you are open, but sometimes like to keep things to yourself."	Client (with a big smile): "That's true."
Childhood Drawing	"I'd like you to go back to a time in your childhood, some memory of your childhood…"	Draws with pastels / crayons / colored pencils	"At your real age, now, what do you notice about this younger child?"	"He's sitting all alone and looking away."
Safe Place Drawing	"I'd like you to imagine that you can go to a safe place…"	Draws with pastels / crayons / colored pencils	Client: "I am this bed… cushioned and supportive…"	Client: "Maybe this is Sonia…she's always there for me."
Rosebush Drawing	"What I'd like you to do is, imagine you are a rosebush, or a flowering bush of any kind…"	Draws with pastels / crayons / colored pencils	"Okay, now be this part you say isn't very perfect. How do other parts feel about that part? If this part could talk, what would it say?"	Therapist: "Well, be the baseball mitt, then. Come back to that." Client: "I'm the baseball mitt…"

Adapted from:
Peter Mortola, *Windowframes*
School of Counseling Psychology
Lewis and Clark College
pmortola@clark.edu

Emotions: Aggressive Energy and Anger

Aggressive Energy

Contacting one's aggressive energy is an important prelude to expressing anger or any other difficult or blocked emotion. This energy provides inner strength for recognizing and getting our needs met. That is, aggressive energy is akin to the kind we use to bite into an apple—it lets us go from a desire to the outward action that fulfills it. Both timid, withdrawn clients and acting-out, seemingly angry clients benefit from acknowledging and releasing aggressive energy in therapeutic activities.

Some essential therapeutic elements must be in place so those activities can help children and adolescents experience their aggressive energy safely and effectively:

1. The client is in contact with the therapist.
2. The child or adolescent feels safe.
3. There are clear limits—the therapist is always in control.
4. There is a spirit of playfulness and fun.
5. The activity is exaggerated.
6. Content is not necessary—it is the *experience* that counts.

Aggressive energy can be expressed through games, bataka fights, pounding clay, music (especially percussion instruments), puppet play, creative dramatics, body movement, sand tray work, written and spoken statements, storytelling and books, and playing with toys—all depending on the age and personality of the child.

The Many Faces of Anger
By Violet Oaklander

Anger is the most misunderstood of all human emotions.

We tend to think of anger as distasteful and abhorrent—something that we would rather not experience. Actually, I believe that the anger is an expression of the self. It is a protection of one's boundaries. When a young child says, "NO!" in a loud voice, mobilizing all the energy she has to express the dislike of something that offends her in some way, she is not angry as we have come to know it, she is expressing her very self. She must use a loud voice because she desperately wants to be heard. Her "NO!" Comes from the core of her being. Since the child does not have cognitive ability, the language, nor the diplomacy to express profound, basic feelings in pleasing ways, she is perceived as angry.

The child soon learns this kind of expression is unacceptable—that he may, if he continues to express the self in this vein, be in danger of abandonment. Since his survival depends on the adults in his life, he will make determinations about how to be in this world to ensure his needs are met. The child's self becomes diminished due to lack of expression, his deep-felt feelings become buried inside of him.

Since the child's major task is to grow up, a paradox takes form. As the child strives to flourish and thrive in her confusing world by calculating how to avoid her parent's disapproval and wrath, her organism struggles to achieve equilibrium and health. And so the expression of anger, this expression of self that has been frustrated and thwarted pushes on to become something else—something beyond the child's awareness and control.

One child retroflects the anger energy by giving herself headaches or stomachaches, generally withdrawing, not speaking, or manifesting other self-inflicted symptoms. Another child will deflect the true feelings by hitting, kicking, striking out. Some children become hyperactive as a way to avoid feeling anything. Others anesthetize themselves and space out. These are only a few of the behaviors and symptoms that mask fearful authentic expressions. These behaviors and symptoms are actually the child's fierce attempts to cope and survive in this stressful world. These inappropriate and unsatisfactory behaviors and symptoms are the many faces of anger.

Expressing Anger

Therapeutic Steps for Children and Adolescents

1. **Awareness:** Talking about Anger
   A. What is it?
   B. What are different kinds of angry feelings?
   C. What makes you angry?
   D. How do you know when you're angry?
   E. How do you show it?

2. **Expressing and Containing One's Aggressive Energy**
   A. Building self-support
   B. Using games, drawings, clay, music, creative dynamics (The Person You Need To Say It To), puppets, stories and books, sand tray work, lists, body movement, statements

3. **Acknowledging one's own rage: "I'm angry!"**

4. **Accepting the Anger:** "It's O.K. that I'm angry. There's no right or wrong about it."

5. **Choosing How to Express it:** Learning new skills to cope with angry feelings:
   A. Direct expression—saying what you need to say
   B. Private expression—Expressing anger in a safe way promotes health and calm.

6. **Working Through Unexpressed Anger**
   A. Being in contact with therapist
   B. A "safe container" of clear limits
   C. A sense of play
   D. Exaggeration

NOTE: Essential for Aggressive Energy Work: Contact, not Content!

Materials & Tools:

- Paper : Newsprint / Printer Paper / Drawing Pad
- Tools : Chalk / Pastels / Crayons / Colored Pencils
- Hard Surface : Drawing Boards / Paper Pad Backing / Table

Anger Drawing

Explanation:

The anger drawing is an opportunity for children to be encouraged and empowered to go back to a time where they felt anger, or any other strong emotion.

Prompt:

"I'd like you to just get as relaxed as you can. And just go inside yourself and see how you're feeling in there…See how your head feels, and your shoulders, and your arms, your stomach, chest, back [5-second pause]. Wiggle your toes, sometimes we forget that we go all the way down to our toes. Take a deep breath [therapist inhales], hold it… and then let it out…[therapist exhales]. Let's do that a couple more times…[therapist inhales, then exhales a few times; 20-second pause]. I'm going to make a sound, and just listen to the sound as long as you can [ring a chime three times].

I'd like you to go back into your childhood and find a time when something happened that made you feel very angry. Or maybe you don't remember feeling angry, but you felt frightened, or upset, or hurt, or ashamed, or like you were a bad child. Something that happened when you felt angry or one of those other things. It might not be a big thing! It might just be some small thing, but that's okay. It doesn't have to be a major thing. Maybe something that popped into your mind that surprises you."

Additional Anger Drawing Exercises

1. Think of a time you were angry in the past year.
2. Think of a time you were angry in the past month.

Anger Actions List: Expressing Anger Safely

Explanation:

Use this list as a guide to help clients come up with their own anger (actions) lists.

Prompt:

"You should feel better, calmer, more peaceful after expressing your anger safely. Let's think of some ways. [Ask client to suggest anger actions, using first person (I, me, my/mine). Make sure the actions are safe. You may suggest any actions below. Once they have a list, tell them: Be sure to breathe deeply, and to focus on your anger while doing any of these."

Sample anger actions:

- Punch a pillow.
- Have a purposeful temper tantrum.
- Hit a mattress with a tennis racket.
- Tear up magazines.
- Squash a piece of paper and throw it.
- Draw the face of someone you're mad at on paper or cardboard, jump on the picture, tear it up, or scrunch it up and throw it.
- Kick a can.
- Squeeze a towel, especially if wet.
- Throw a wet washcloth against the wall in the bathtub.
- Talk into a tape recorder about your angry feelings.
- Write about your angry feelings.
- Write all the bad words you can think of.
- Write a letter to someone you're mad at and tear it up.
- Scream into a pillow.
- Run around the block or do any other physical activity until you are exhausted, while focusing on your anger.
- Punch clay or Play-Doh with your fist or pound it with a rubber mallet.
- Beat on a drum.

- Do an angry dance to music.
- Smash aluminum cans.
- Growl into a mirror.
- Tape the name of the person you're mad at on the bottom of your shoe, and stomp around.
- Chew gum, imagining you are biting that person, or bite a washcloth.
- Throw rocks into the ocean or other safe place.
- Spray a water gun or spray bottle, imagining it's at a person you're mad at.
- Throw ice cubes at a wall and yell and scream.
- Stuff a pillowcase or grocery bag with grass, draw a face on it, hit it.
- Hit a tin trash can with a baseball bat.
- Throw balloons filled with water.
- Collect twigs and sticks, and break them.

> **ANGER LIST**
>
> 1. Growl into a mirror.
> 2. Tape bottom of shoe with name of person you are mad at and walk around.
> 3. Chew Gum - imagine you are biting person; or bite washcloth.
> 4. Throw rocks - into ocean or other safe place.
> 5. Spray at a person (imaginary) with a water gun or spray bottle.

Materials & Tools:

- Clay
- Clay board and Clay tools
- Water / Paper towels / Wipes

Clay Work: Something from Nothing Activity

Explanation:

This projective activity is an opportunity to give children sensory contact and experience with clay in a non-threatening way.

Prompt:

"I'd like you to just get as relaxed as you can. And just go inside yourself and see how you're feeling in there… See how your head feels, and your shoulders, and your arms, your stomach, chest, back [5-second pause]. Wiggle your toes, sometimes we forget that we go all the way down to our toes. Take a deep breath [therapist inhales], hold it…and then let it out…[therapist exhales]. Let's do that a couple more times…[therapist inhales and exhales a few times; 20-second pause]. I'm going to make a sound, and just listen to the sound as long as you can [ring chime three times].

Okay, now I want you to make a lump, just a lump, and put it in front of you…put your hands over it. And what I would like you to do is close your eyes and feel the temperature of the clay with the palms of your hands…Take a deep breath and when you exhale, imagine the air going down through your arms, down your fingers, into the clay. Do that a few times.

I want you to try an experiment: Feel the clay with the palm of your hands with your eyes closed… Now open your eyes and feel the clay with the palms of your hands. Then close your eyes again. Did you notice anything? [Client nods]. I think you can actually feel the clay more with your eyes closed. It's more like your eyes take some of your energy away from it.

Okay, now your clay has a lot of your energy in it; it's even warm where you have been touching it. I would like you to begin to form something. Now, just let the clay go where it wants to go. This might be just an abstract shape. It might be that you want to make some kind of an object or an animal or a figure of some kind. Just try, with your eyes closed, just try to make something, but don't look at it yet. Don't worry about what you are making, just continue working [45-second pause].

And then, anytime you feel like opening your eyes, just go ahead and look at your piece, but just keep working on it. At some point you'll want to open your eyes and just look at it and see it from all sides, see if you want to fix anything. Don't' really change it [60-second pause]. At this point you should open your eyes if they are not open, and put any finishing touches onto what you've just made [30-second pause]. See if you are surprised at what you did [15-second pause]. One of the things about this is that there is no real finishing place. You could sort of keep working and keep working at it, and so you have to say, 'Okay, I'll stop now.'"

Emotions: Grief and Loss

Developmental Issues in Grief and Loss

Children of all ages may suffer many kinds of loss: loss of a grandparent, sibling, friend, or parent through death; loss of a friend, neighborhood, beloved toy, favorite teacher, pet, divorced or separated parent, or their own health.

Children who have been abused or live in dysfunctional families have often lost much of their childhood and have missed many experiences needed for their healthy development.

Specific issues to expect when working with young clients experiencing loss:

1. Confusion
2. Sense of abandonment
3. Loss of self-confidence
4. Egocentricity—blaming the self for the loss
5. Guilt—"What did I do wrong?" or "If only I had…."
6. Fear
7. Control
8. Betrayal
9. Unexpressed sadness and anger
10. Isolation: feeling "alone" and "different," closing off the self
11. Shame

Grief at Each Developmental Stage:
Reactions and Best Responses

Infancy to 2 years
No concept of death
React to emotion in others
React to separation from the one who cares for them
Reaction: Crankiness, lots of tears, clinging
Best response: Keep routine intact—they know something is terribly wrong.

3 to 5 years
Age of discovery: use all their senses
No abstract thinking, hear but cannot interpret information
No concept of death for self
Think they have the power to kill
Egocentric: blame the self for the distress
Believe death is reversible as seen on TV, movies, children's play
Reaction: Wanting to fix things; magical thinking
Best response: Telling the truth; repetition

6 to 9 years
They know they can die—they fear death
Reaction: Anxiety
Best response: Lots of reassurance

10 to 13 years
Death is very personal; they have a realistic view of death
Reaction: Curiosity about the biological aspects of death
Separation anxiety
Grades fall
Hold in feelings and develop inappropriate behaviors
Emotional pulling away as defense and self-preservation mechanism
Best response: Telling the truth; accepting them despite their acting out while maintaining boundaries and limits

Adolescence

Reaction: Anxiety about own death

Emotional withdrawal from family and friends as unconscious self-protective strategy

Occasionally, anger at dead person or others

Occasionally, maturation and supportiveness

Best response: Normalizing grief reactions

Materials & Tools:

- Paper : Newsprint / Printer Paper / Drawing Pad
- Tools : Chalk / Pastels / Crayons / Colored Pencils
- Hard Surface : Drawing Boards / Paper Pad Backing / Table

Grief Drawing

Explanation:

This drawing gives children an opportunity to imagine and draw their feelings about a loved one who has died. They then can process their feelings in therapy using this projective piece.

Prompt:

"I'd like you to just get as relaxed as you can. And just go inside yourself and see how you're feeling in there…. See how your head feels, and your shoulders, and your arms, your stomach, chest, back [5-second pause]. Wiggle your toes, sometimes we forget that we go all the way down to our toes. Take a deep breath [therapist inhales], hold it…and then let it out … [therapist exhales]. Let's do that a couple more times … [therapist inhales and exhales a few times; 20-second pause]. I'm going to make a sound, and just listen to the sound as long as you can [therapist rings a chime three times]."

Grief Projects

1. **Loved One Drawing:** Ask the client to draw a picture of the loved one they are grieving.
2. **Memory Book:** Ask the client to make a memory book of the person they are grieving.

Guide to Brief Therapy

1. **Set priorities.** List the issues involved in the situation, then focus on the most important work.

2. **Cut to the chase.** Go right to the fear, grief, anger. Get the feelings out. Don't be afraid—get right in there.

3. **See it as a crisis.** Create a sense of urgency by telling the child or adolescent you have only a few sessions to make things better.

4. **Immediately establish an I-Thou relationship and a sense of safety with the child or adolescent.** Be genuine. Respect and honor the client. Meet the client where they are—be **contactful** with the client. **DO NOT HAVE ANY EXPECTATIONS** of establishing the relationship or not based solely on the brevity of the time.

5. **Look at the number of sessions.** Plan what you will do. For example, spend first session on the relationship.

6. **Structure the anger work and do it.** Be sure to tell the child or adolescent what you are doing.

7. **Try the self-nurturing process as soon as possible.**

8. **Teach parents how to do the work.** Explain the therapy process so they can help.

9. **Show parents how anger work and self-nurturing work happen.**

10. **Stress limit-setting.** Set safe and fair boundaries with parents.

11. **Solutions:** Have child or adolescent choose one behavior, situation or symptom they want to improve or change. Discuss options. Plan experiments.

12. **Pick activities at client's developmental level.** Explain this concept to parents.

13. **Keep in mind that therapy is always intermittent with children and adolescents.** Termination is generally temporary.

14. **Keep in mind that something important happens in each session.**

15. **Remember that you can't fix everything.** You can only do what you can do. You can't push the river.

Materials & Tools:

- Varies, activity can be drawing, clay, puppets, creative dramatics, sand tray, etc.

Polarities

Examples:

WEAK/STRONG

ALONE/TOGETHER

HAPPY/SAD

OPEN/CLOSED

INNER/OUTER

BRAVE/AFRAID

GOOD/BAD

FOUND/LOST

SERIOUS/SILLY

SMART/DUMB

AGGRESSIVE/PASSIVE

SANE/CRAZY

SUPERIOR/INFERIOR

LOVE/HATE

Suggested Activities Prompts:

You get the idea! There are many, many more polarities. Explore and help children and adolescents integrate polarities within themselves through:

Drawing: "Draw how it feels to be happy and then sad."

Clay: "Make an image of yourself when you're weak and then when you're strong."

Puppets: "Pick a puppet that is good and one that is bad. What do they say to each other?"

Creative Dramatics: "Show how you walk, play tennis, or do anything else when you feel passive, then aggressive."

Sand Tray: "Make a scene that is serious, then one that is silly."

Materials & Tools:
- Puppets

Puppet Work

Suggested Activities Prompts:

1. The therapist always chooses a puppet to "be" to start the activity. Violet often chose the "wise owl" for her puppet.

2. Pick a puppet that represents now **you feel right now** (tired, crazy, happy, angry).

3. Pick a puppet that would be the **opposite** of how you feel right now.

4. Pick a puppet that reminds you of a part of yourself that you **don't like.**

5. Pick a puppet that represents how you would **like to be.**

6. Pick puppets that represent **your family.** Introduce them. Where would you place them? What would you like to say to each person? Say something you like and something you don't like. Tell them how you wish they would be.

7. Pick a puppet that represents your **secret inner voice** that knows things.

8. Pick a puppet that's **angry.**

9. Focus the client on **polarities:** weak/strong, happy/sad, etc.

10. Tell the client a **metaphorical story** using puppets, related to the client's conflict, fears, anxieties, or life.

11. Using puppets, **tell the client a story that needs a solution, and ask the client** what to do.

12. Tell the client you'll put on a puppet show, **and ask the client for a theme.**

13. Have the client do a puppet show **giving them a theme.**

14. Use puppets **with a family:** Each member picks one and each **talks to the others.** Or have them **create and do a show. Watch the process**—it will tell you a lot about the family dynamics.

15. **In groups**: Have each client pick a puppet and introduce it; then have the puppet introduce the client. Puppets dialogue with each other. Therapist's puppet is in control.

Types of puppets Violet recommends:

Family figures, (though Violet also likes to use animals or character puppets for these), a witch, a wizard or magician, a king, a queen, a prince and a princess, an old man and an old woman, a devil, a police-man, a fairy godmother, a doctor, a judge, a ghost; cute and cuddly animals as a teddy bear, dog, kitten, rabbit; and fierce animals as a shark, wolf, alligator and such; and it's good to have a couple of "neutral" puppets such as an owl, and a turtle is a good one since it can hide in its shell. Also, one or two "silly" puppets.

Of course, there are many other puppets you could have. I have so many, and there's always one I need that I don't have. It's important to have puppets that represent polarities (good and bad). Avoid stereotypical puppets, if possible.

Children can make puppets out of paper bags, socks or other materials.

Ways to use puppets:

Puppets are great in groups. Each child picks a puppet, introduces self, and begins to talk to each other. The therapist guides the process with his or her chosen puppet. Mine is often the wise owl. Sometimes, I may ask the puppet to tell me things about the child.

Stuffed animals can be used as puppets.

The therapist generally talks to the puppets, or the child, using a puppet. Puppets can say things that might be outrageous if the therapist said them.

Children like to put on their own show using a puppet theater or behind a chair.

Violet has had children add musical instruments to puppet shows, directing them by pointing to the desired instrument to play during various parts of the show.

Sometimes a fantasy story or game is developed when the child has a puppet and then the therapist has a puppet. You sit on the floor and go from there. The child develops the story. You may say, "What should my puppet say?" "What should they (my puppet) do now?", etc.

EXAGGERATE AND HAVE FUN!

Table 2: Violet's Prompts for Metaphoric or Narrative Description

	Imaginary Experience **IMAGINE IT**	Sensory Experience **MAKE IT**	Metaphoric Narrative Articulation **BE IT**	Sense Making Application **DOES THIS FIT?**
Anger Drawing	"Find a time when something happened that made you feel angry."	Client draws a picture with crayons, markers or pastels.	Client role-plays various parts of the picture: "I am this hammer, pointed at everybody else."	Client: "Yes, I'm still in similar situations," or "It used to, but not anymore."
Grief Drawing	"Think about your loved one who died."	Client draws a picture of the feeling they have of missing the person.	Client role-plays the parts of the picture: "That's me in the background because my mom is gone."	Client: "It is how I feel missing him," or "That's what I wish he could have said to me (or I wish I could have said to him)."
Puppet Work	"I would like you to pick a puppet for each member of your family."	Client picks a puppet for each member of the family.	Client role-plays each puppet, or tells each puppet one thing they like about the puppet and one thing they don't like about the puppet."	Client: "My sister is just like this unicorn, very different from everyone else."

Adapted from:
Peter Mortola, *Windowframes*
School of Counseling Psychology
Lewis and Clark College
pmortola@clark.edu

Materials & Tools:
- Cards

Picture Cards

Explanation:

Picture cards can be used as a projective activity for children. They are particularly helpful for children who don't like to draw, or when you are short on time.

Suggested Activities Prompts:

1. Pick three animals: One that's how you see yourself now—one that fits you now; a second one that's how you saw yourself in the past and didn't like—that you don't want to be; and a third one that's how you would like to be—what you want to be like. Tell me about them. [Prompt as needed:] Why do you want to be (or don't want to be) like this one? Write down responses.
2. Draw: Put animals in the drawing doing something together someplace, and anything else you want in the picture.
3. Work with the pictures: Invite client to be an animal, to talk with the animal/s, to have animals talk together, to create a story, to relate the story to their life.
4. Pick animals that stand for people in your family.
5. One animal may be chosen for dream animal or protector or guide.

Notes:

- If response to "Tell me about them" is "I don't know," move to doing the drawing.
- Some clients might choose the same card for more than one response.
- Clients often perceive themselves as viewed from the outside, not from their own inside view.

The cards suggested to use for this model are any pictures that can be used to elicit projective responses. It is recommended that the cards you use are without any writing on them, to facilitate the client's own projection onto the cards.

The pictures can be of animals, city scenes, scenes in nature, inside spaces, people, etc. that you find in magazines and cut out and laminate for future use. Many therapists use Medicine Cards, Oh Cards, the Dixit card game and various versions of tarot decks of cards. Oaklandertraining.org has online Projective Cards.

Materials & Tools:

- Tray : With sand evenly distributed as a blank canvas.
- Tools : Range of Miniatures / Toys / Natural objects / etc. (see page 67).
- Scenes : Have on hand water, tin foil, plastic wrap, string, wire, masking tape, sticks, small plastic plants, etc.

Sand Tray Work

Explanation:

The Oaklander Method uses sand tray and miniatures for children to create scenes as projections of their inner experience, wishes, feelings, and/or past, present and future situations in their lives.

Prompt:

"I would like you to make a scene in the sand. You can use any of the objects you see here and, if there's something you don't see, ask me—maybe I have it. Your scene doesn't have to make sense, or it can. You can choose things because you like them and want to use them. Or you might want to make something special. It can be real or imaginary or like a dream. Anything.

[If useful, show the child or adolescent photographs of sand trays to give them the idea of what you mean.]

[You may also ask the client to do a special theme, asking:] Do a scene representing the divorce in your family [or] How do you feel these days? [or] Show something that represents opposites, using both trays—happy/sad, war/peace—any set of opposites."

What to Observe and How to Respond:

Levels of Sand Tray Work

Some therapists use sand trays to assess clients' process, emotional feel, and functional age. Yet even informal observation can tell you a lot.

1. **Process:** Note the client's energy level: Are they slow and methodical or fast and frenzied? Do they change their mind many times? Do they need everything close at hand that they think they might want, even though things are right on the shelves? Does the client use only a few objects or many? Do they spend a lot of time feeling or smoothing the sand? Do they use a lot of water?

2. **The general look of the tray:** Observe its organization. Is it compulsively organized? Chaotic? Are things just stuck in with no organizations at all? Is it an angry-looking scene? A peaceful one?

3. **Symbolic level:** Yes, there is one, but interpretation can get the therapist into quicksand, so just keep it experiential!

4. **The field:** What is the tray's general environmental look?

5. **Making-sense level:** Children and adolescents always attempt to make sense out of the scene, just as they try to make sense of their lives. You may say, "Tell me about your scene." They'll look at it and then say, "Well, this is a …."

6. **Metaphorical level:** Developing a story out of the scene.

7. **Acting out various objects:** You may say, "Be that lion, and tell me about yourself. Just say, 'I'm a lion….'" [Client:] "I'm a lion." [Therapist:] "Hello, lion. Where are you? What are you doing? What do you want to do?"

8. **Dialoguing:** The client engages in a dialogue with two or more parts. [Therapist:] "What does the lion say to the tiger? What does the tiger say back? If the tree could talk, what would it say to the lion?"

9. **Owning:** Ask, "Does anything here remind you of you or anything in your life?" or "Do you ever feel like you need a place to hide like the rabbit in your story?"

10. **Changing the scene:** Ask the client to move objects or activate them: "Make the war happen." "Where would you like to put that figure?"

11. **Getting the existential message:** Ask, "What does this whole thing tell you about yourself and your life?"

12. **Pay attention to the client's energy.**

Sand Tray Resources

Sand tray catalogs

Aquarium stores

Cake decorating stores or sites

Party shops or sites

Toy stores or sites

Floral decorating stores (trees, bushes, etc.)

Flea markets, garage sales

Drug stores

Theme parks, zoo, aquarium, museum gift shops

Model train stores

Craft stores

Self-Acceptance and Self-Nurturing

Even a young child, particularly if disturbed, has a well-developed critical self, taking everything personally and turning everything back against the self. They develop powerful negative introjects—internalized unconscious images of the self—and often do a better job of critique than their parents do. This judgmental stance, while often invisible to others, hurts healthy growth.

The child may vow, "I will be better," but enacting this wish is beyond their power and comprehension. The will to "be better" often only intensifies despair. Each trauma, large or small, takes its toll on the child by fomenting unexpressed feelings—"unfinished business"—and especially self-blame. The child develops a negative belief about them that can never be changed by any outside agent.

Yet self-acceptance of all one's parts, even the most hateful, is vital to unimpaired, sound development. Self-acceptance comes about through the strengthening of a nurturing self. The youngster's own loving, nurturing part must meet with the "bad" self to accept, understand, comfort, and love it. The child who comes to accept and to experience all aspects of herself or himself without judgment grows joyfully.

Through self-nurturing work, we dig out those darker views of the self, illuminate them, and bring them into contact with the client's nurturing self, so they can finally experience integration.

Self-Nurturing Work

1. Working with the Introjects

   A. Normalize: "We all have parts of ourselves we don't like."

   B. Explore them with projective activities: drawings, clay, stories, drama, symbols, or other media.

   C. With the client, choose one specific part to work with. Focus on the specific rather than the general.

   D. Have the client personify and elaborate on the hateful part using drawings, imagery, clay, puppets, creative dramatics, and other techniques.

   E. Help the client get in touch with their anger at the part. Since an introject is a retroflection (a turning against oneself), expressing anger at the part when bringing it outward prepares one for self-nurturing work.

   F. If the client is old enough to have a sense of time, explore the origin or the initial age of the part; "How long has it been with you?"

   G. To reveal the negative introject, you may look at the polar, idealized part.

2. The Self-Nurturing Process

   A. Find the nurturer within the client's self—the nurturing part. This is expressed as a projection at first: The client, for example, can find a puppet to represent the "fairy godmother" or some other loving figure who will speak to the hateful part.

   B. If the hateful part character is much younger, the client can speak to that part, which is actually the little girl or boy who swallowed the introject.

   C. When a projection is used, such as the fairy godmother or any chosen nurturing character, the client speaks to the hateful part as himself or herself, using words similar to those of the nurturer. The therapist always checks, "How does it feel to say that to yourself?"

   D. If needed, model the nurturer part for the client.

3. **Giving Homework**
   A. After practicing this "assignment" in the office, ask the child or adolescent to find something at home that represents the younger part that feels bad and to say to it, every night, with a hug, the nurturing statements you've practiced.
   B. Make a list of nice things the client can do independently. Ask them to do one of these things every day, and to report back on what they did and how it felt.
   C. Remind the child or adolescent to call forth the fairy godmother (or other nurturing character) whenever they feel bad about something they did or that happened.

Excerpted from *Hidden Treasure*
A Map To The Child's Inner Self

Materials & Tools:

- Paper : Newsprint / Printer Paper / Drawing Pad
- Tools : Chalk / Pastels / Crayons / Colored Pencils
- Hard Surface : Drawing Boards / Paper Pad Backing / Table

Demon Drawing*

Explanation:

The demon drawing is used in the self-nurturing process as a fun and accessible way for children to identify and work with parts of themselves that they don't like.

*You can substitute the word **demon** for a part of the self that you don't like.*

Prompt:

"I'd like you to just get as relaxed as you can. And just go inside yourself and see how you're feeling in there…. See how your head feels, and your shoulders, and your arms, your stomach, chest, back [5-second pause]. Wiggle your toes, sometimes we forget that we go all the way down to our toes. Take a deep breath [therapist inhales], hold it…and then let it out … [therapist exhales]. Let's do that a couple more times … [therapist inhales and exhales a few times; 20-second pause]. I'm going to make a sound, and just listen to the sound as long as you can [therapist rings a chime three times].

So, what I'm going to ask you to do, and I know we all have several demons, is think about one of your demons. It could be a part of yourself that you don't like, or that gets in the way sometimes. It doesn't have to be totally horrible and it could be something that is not bad, but something you still wish you didn't have. It could be any one you think of. You can do it anyway you want to draw. It can be very abstract, just colors and shapes if you want. It doesn't have to be artistic, as I keep saying.

Just express your own demon using whatever you want. Then name your demon, give it a name on the page. So that's what I'd like you to do right now."

Examples of Demons or parts of the self you don't like

The self-pity demon
The spacing-out demon
The demon who thinks too much
The anger demon
The egocentric demon
The speed demon
The foolhardy demon
The messy demon
The demon of pride
The afraid-to-be-himself demon
The paranoid demon
The despair demon
The demon of fear
The procrastination demon
The demon who lies
The shattered demon
The demon of snobbery
The obsession demon
The compulsion demon
The demon of time
The hunger demon
The ambitious demon
The demon of lethargy
The broken-hearted demon
The gossip demon
The loneliness demon
The demon who makes you draw demons
The demon slayer

Demons by Randy La Chapelle
Pure Diamond Press 1975

Table 3: Violet's Prompts for Metaphoric or Narrative Description

	Imaginary Experience **IMAGINE IT**	Sensory Experience **MAKE IT**	Metaphoric Narrative Articulation **BE IT**	Sense Making Application **DOES THIS FIT?**
Picture Cards	"Pick three cards that represent how you are, were and would like to be."	Client picks 3 cards and places them in order of past, present and future.	Client role-plays each card: "I'm the owl…."	Client: "I'm happy that in my future I use what I learned."
Sand Tray	"I would like you to make a scene in the sand…it can be real or imaginary, like a dream."	Client makes a sand tray scene using a variety of toys or natural objects.	Client plays the parts of the items in the scene, and dialogs with and among them.	Client "owns" the projections onto the scene: "That sounds a lot like me."
Demon Drawing	"Think about one of your demons."	Client identifies as, then draws, her or his demon with pastels, crayons or markers.	Client: "I'm the procrastinating demon."	Client: "Yes, I hate that I put off my work and then have to rush to finish."

Adapted from:
Peter Mortola, *Windowframes*
School of Counseling Psychology
Lewis and Clark College
pmortola@clark.edu

Materials & Tools:

- Variety of Musical Instruments / Musical Toys

Music Process

Explanation:

The Oaklander Model uses musical instruments as another way to be playful, have contact with the senses and express and work with emotions. There are four formats:
1. Working with a small group
2. Working with an individual
3. Working with a family
4. Working with a large group

Prompts:

1. Working with a small group

   A. Four or five people sit on the floor around a pile of instruments; any others in the room sit facing the small group. Each person in the small group tries out the instruments and finally selects two.

   B. Begin with a short meditation for everyone and a short silence. Then say, "Those in the outside group, keep your eyes closed and listen—tune into the sounds, the images, and the feelings you experience."

   C. Then ask the small group, "Can someone make a sound? Everyone can join in when they want. Remember, it's not about rhythm or melody—we're just making sounds much like we hear in nature. Make your own sound, maybe along with someone, or stay silent for a while. Make loud or soft sounds—variation is key. If you want, choose another instrument. Stay in touch with what's going on inside you."

   D. Usually the group ends spontaneously, but the therapist may need to whisper to the group, "Now it's time to stop."

2. Working with an individual

The client chooses an instrument and plays for a few moments. The therapist listens, then picks an instrument and joins in. The client stops and the therapist continues alone. The client listens, chooses another instrument, and joins in. Then the therapist stops and listens to the client play. Repeat pattern: solo play while other listens; play together, switch person and instrument to solo play while other listens; play together.

Variations with individuals

- Both therapist and client play together, choosing instruments to play feelings (angry, alive, anxious, sad, crazy, happy).
- Continuation Story: Therapist starts a story while client plays an instrument, then client continues the story while therapist plays.
- Fantasy: Both play while therapist narrates a fantasy. For example: "Close your eyes and imagine you're at the beach. Someone is flying a kite. The kite soars high. It rises and dips. Suddenly it falls to the sand."

3. Working with a family

Try small group and individual formats; both work well.

4. Working with a large group

Each person chooses an instrument. One person plays alone for a bit, then a second joins in, then each person joins in until all are playing together. Rhythms and melody are OK. Encourage people to get up and move, they may use mouth and body sounds, too. After a while, ask the first person to stop playing, followed by the second, then the third and so on until all stop.

Termination According to the Oaklander Model

- Parents might resist therapy for their children because they fear it will be a prolonged time.
- While some children do need long-term treatment, as a general rule this model is relatively short-term.
    - -In general, children haven't accumulated a lot of unfinished business.
    - -Three to six months of concentrated therapy might warrant termination.
- In cases of significant trauma may require more long-term treatment.
- Children reach a plateau in therapy, and this can be a good stopping place.
    - -Can be an opportunity to integrate, and assimilate with their own natural maturation and growth, the changes taking place as the result of the therapy.
    - -Sometimes this plateau is a sign of resistance that needs to be respected. It's as if the child knows they cannot handle breaking through this particular wall at this time. They need more time, more strength; they may need to open up to this particular place when they are older. Children seem to have an inner sense of this fact, and the therapist needs to recognize the difference between this stopping place and previous stumbling blocks.
- Clues for knowing when it's time to stop:
    - -The child's behavior has changed, as reported by the school and their parents.
    - -Suddenly they become involved in outside activities – baseball, clubs, friends.
    - -Therapy begins to get in the way of their life.
    - -After the initial wariness, and until such a plateau is reached, the child generally looks forward to coming to the sessions. If they don't, one needs to take a close look at what's happening.
- Improved behavior alone may not be reason enough to stop the therapy. Changed behavior can be due to the child's opening up and expressing a deeper self to the therapist. The material that comes through in the sessions can be good indicators of stopping places.
- Preparing a child for termination is important. Though we help kids gain as much independence and self-support as we can, we certainly do form caring attachments with each other. We need to deal with the feelings involved in saying good-bye to anyone we like and care about.

- Termination need not have the finality that the name implies. Termination is merely a coming to a stopping place, an ending at this time. Some children need reassurance that they will be able to come back if they need to (if indeed it is possible).
- Termination in schools can include a picture, in colors, lines and shapes, of what it feels like now to be leaving this classroom?
- We always have some unfinished business about separation and good-byes that makes termination that much more difficult. We need to be in touch with our own feelings at such times and not be afraid to express them honestly. There's nothing wrong with being sad (or for that matter, glad) over a leave-taking!

Excerpted from *Hidden Treasure*
A Map To The Child's Inner Self

Supplemental Activities

Materials & Tools:

- Paper : Poster Board / Heavy Stock / Drawing Pad
- Tools : Pastels / Crayons / Colored Pencils
- Hard Surface : Drawing Boards / Paper Pad Backing / Table

Coat of Arms Drawing

Explanation:

The Coat of Arms is a fun and more cognitive exercise to allow children and adolescents to make self-statements. This strengthens their sense of self-one of the primary goals of the therapeutic process.

Prompt:

Make Your Personal Crest!

Put your name or motto in the ribbon, and represent with symbols or pictures:

1. One thing you do well.
2. One thing that is important to you.
3. Three things you would take if your house were on fire, your family and pets were safe, and you had only 10 minutes.
4. Your greatest accomplishment.
5. A person you admire.
6. One thing you would change if you had all the power in the world.

Coat of Arms Template

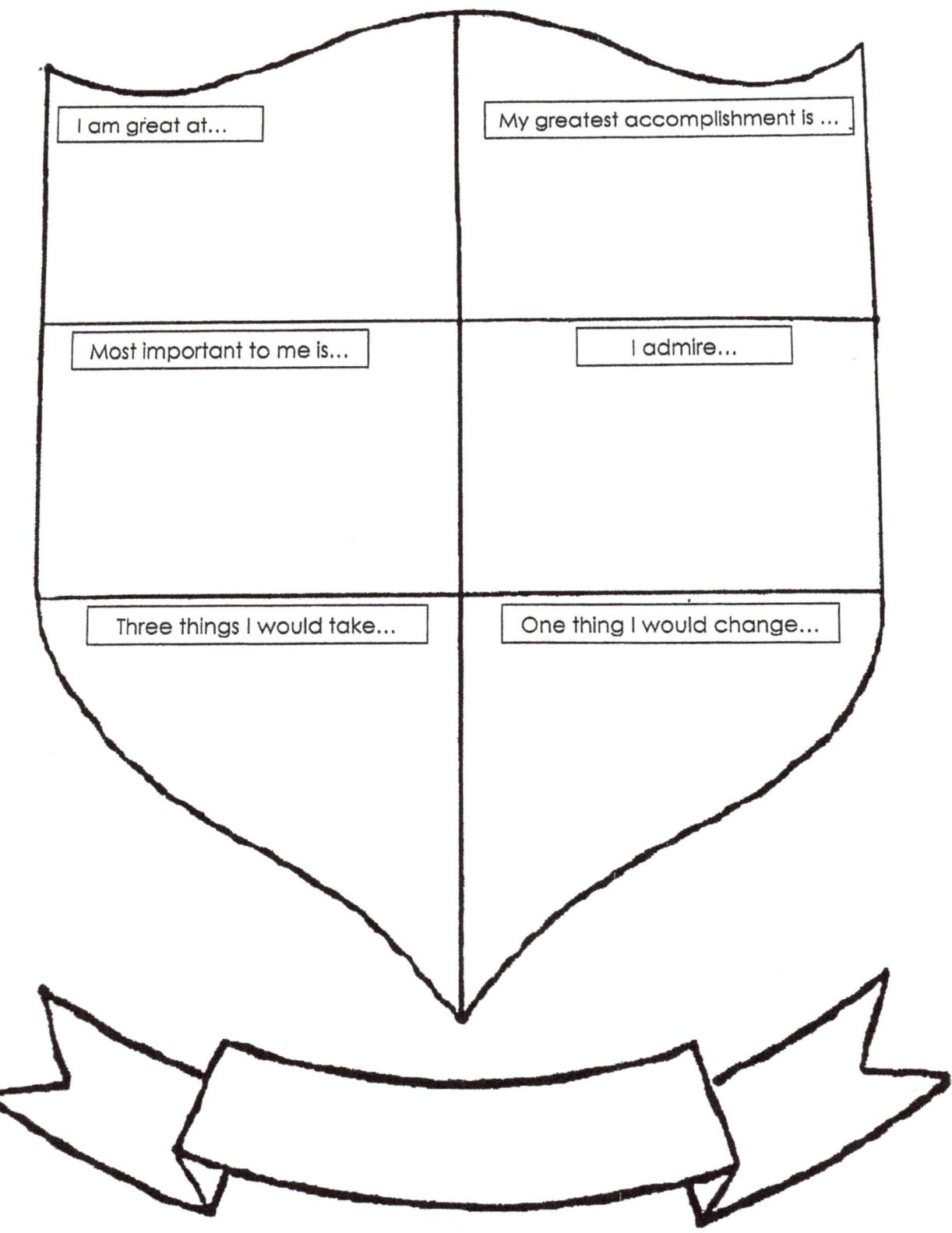

Materials & Tools:

- Paper : Newsprint / Printer Paper / Drawing Pad
- Tools : Markers (At Least 2)
- Hard Surface : Drawing Boards / Paper Pad Backing / Table

Scribble Drawing

Explanation:

In *Windows to Our Children*, Violet describes this drawing experience as "…a very unthreatening method to help children express outwardly something of their inner selves." (p. 37)

Prompt:

"I'd like you to stand up with one marker in your dominant hand (keep the cap on). Imagine a piece of paper that is the height of your body, out to the sides of you and ending at your feet. You are going to draw a scribble on this imaginary piece of paper. I am going to count to ten, and you are going to draw your scribble in the air with me. Your shape will vary. Imagine you start at the top of the paper, and imagine drawing all the way down. I am going to count to ten and you are going to draw an imaginary scribble. Ready? [Count to 10 slowly.]

And now go to your real piece of paper, and make that design from top to bottom on your real paper with your marker. Be quick, whatever your scribble was, that's what you reproduce on your paper, top to bottom.

Now put that first marker aside. Look at your scribble, and you're going to make something out of it. Using your second marker, make something recognizable. It could be anything. [Give the client or clients about 5 minutes to draw the scribble creation. Then, invite the client or clients to share what they made.]"

Exercises to Strengthen the Self

Explanation:

These exercises strengthen the client's sense of self through contact with their senses and breath.

Prompts:

Touch

- Without being seen, place objects in a bag and ask client to describe their textures, then to guess what each is by feel alone.
- Invite client to finger paint; handle wet clay; sift sand with hands.
- Ask client to list words describing sensations from touch (bumpy, fluffy, slippery, hard, soft, smooth, sticky, gooey, warm, cold, hot, freezing, rough, holes, prickly, tingly, feathery, rubbery, thin, spongy, mushy, silky, hairy).
- Ask client to match colors to these sensation words.
- Ask client to draw pictures to represent these words.

Hearing

- Have client meditate on whatever sounds come into awareness.
- Have client paint while listening to music.
- Ask client to make loud and soft sounds, higher and lower sounds with instruments.
- Have a "conversation" just with sounds, not words.
- Play a game of recognizing sounds.
- Ask client to match sounds with feelings.

Sight

- Play "Where's Waldo?"
- Have client look at very detailed pictures.
- Invite client to draw, paint, or sketch flowers, fruit, trees.
- Have client touch items with eyes closed, then open.
- Ask client to look at things through glass, water, cellophane, magnifiers, a kaleidoscope.

Smell

- Talk about favorite and less-favorite smells.
- Pantomime smells of various things for the other person to guess.
- Tell of experiences with various scents (fruit, hay, cookies, ocean).
- Without being seen, put distinctly fragranced items in opaque containers (perfume, mustard, cinnamon, vinegar) and ask the client to describe and guess each.

Taste

- Do the orange exercise (in *Windows to Our Children,* pp. 266).
- Discuss favorite and not-so-favorite tastes.
- Bring in samples of things to taste, and compare tastes and textures.
- Pantomime eating different foods.

Body-Breath-Voice

- Experiment with different ways to breathe (fast, slow, through mouth, then nose).
- Blow up balloons and keep them in the air with breath.
- Race cotton balls across a table by blowing on them.
- Play the harmonica.
- Role-play various voices.
- Have a yelling contest.

References

Hammer, F., Buck, J., and Jolles, I. (1964-1968). *The House-Tree-Person (H-T-P): Projective Technique.* Los Angeles, CA: Western Psychological Services.

Mortola, P. (2006). *Windowframes: Learning the Art of Gestalt Play Therapy the Oaklander Way.* Santa Cruz, CA: Gestalt Press.

Oaklander, V. (2006). *Hidden Treasure: A Map to the Child's Inner Self.* London: Karmac Books.

Oaklander, V. (1978). *Windows to our Children: A Gestalt Therapy Approach to Children and Adolescents.* Highland, NY: The Gestalt Journal Press.

Perls, F. *The Gestalt Approach & Eye Witness to Therapy.* (1973). Ben Lemond, California: Science and Behavior Books.

Polster, E. and Polster, M. *Gestalt Therapy Integrated: Contours of Theory and Practice.* (1973). New York : Brunnel/Mazel.

Appendix

Assessment

1. **Ability to form a relationship**
   Do they play well with others?
   Do they have friends?
   Do they respect your limits and boundaries?
   Do you trust they will observe them?
   Can they share?

2. **Contact: ability to be present (assess family)**
   Are you and the client present with each other?
   If so, can they maintain it?
   Can they appropriately withdraw?

3. **Contact skills**
   How can your client use their contact modalities?
   Seeing
   Listening
   Smelling
   Talking (spoken language)
   Moving (using the body to communicate)

4. **Aliveness**
   Do you note involvement, interest, animation, excitement, or lack of these?
   Is their voice expressive or flat?
   Does it have volume, or is it barely audible?
   How does the client use their breath?
   What is the client's energy level?
   When does that level vary?

5. **Body**
   How do they walk, stand, sit?
   Does the body appear restricted or loose and flexible?
   What is their posture like? Are their shoulders hunched?

6. **Humor**
   Does the client respond to your and others' humor and exhibit their own sense of humor?

7. **Expression and Affect**
   Do they know what feelings are? Do they have a varied feelings vocabulary?
   Do they manifest affect in some way when it is appropriate; that is, are they congruent with what they feel and how they expresses it?
   Are they able to express their feelings?
   How do they handle emotions at home, at school and with friends?
   In particular, what do they do with their angry feelings?
   Do they have old, unexpressed, unfinished feelings of grief or anger (or both)?
   Are their reactions in proportion to the problem?

8. **Cognitive abilities**
   Can they express/articulate feelings and thoughts?
   How are their language skills? Does the client have speech or language problems of any kind?
   Can they follow directions, play a game, make choices, solve problem situations, organize?
   Do they have ideas, opinions?
   Does what they say make sense?
   Do they understand and use abstractions and symbols appropriate to their age?
   Do they have a sense of "right and wrong?"

9. **Creativity**
   Are they able to be open, participate in creative techniques, try new things – or are they closed, restricted, armored, highly defended?

10. **Sense of self**
    Does the client have some introspection or self-awareness?
    Can they "own" their projections produced by various projective techniques?
    Does the client appear to devalue self?
    Are they self-critical?
    Do they appear insecure about self or constantly seek approval?
    Can the client make "self" statements: "This is what I want/what I don't want/like/don't like." Can they make choices?
    Does the client seem particularly needy?
    Do they appear assertive or meek and timid?
    Are they able to separate from their parents?
    Does the client exhibit confluent (merged) behavior?
    Do they fight for power?
    Does the client have a sense of mastery appropriate to their age?

11. Social skills
How does the client relate to others in their life? Do they have friends?
Do they show signs of independent thinking and action?
Can they find outside support for what they need? How is this accomplished?

12. Process
How does the client present themselves in the world—quiet, noisy, aggressive, passive, fearful, "very good," mischievous, sickly, immature, mature, a leader or a follower, moody, overly cheerful?
What are they like with you, siblings, friends, teachers?
What problematic behaviors do they exhibit?

Assessment Worksheet

Contact Functions

_____
_____
_____
_____

Aliveness/Body/Energy

_____
_____
_____
_____

Expression

_____
_____
_____
_____

Cognitive Abilities

_____
_____
_____
_____

Creativity

_____
_____
_____
_____

Sense of Self

Relationship with Parents, as Observed

Behavioral Manifestations at Home, as Reported

Behavioral Manifestations in Office, as Observed

Client's General Process

Treatment Recommended

Treatment Plan

Violet taught that the easiest way to set up a treatment plan is to follow the assessment categories. But these need to be understood in the context of child development, following models of growth stages such as Erik Erikson's holistic one and Piaget's theory of intellectual maturation. Equally essential is focusing on a client's unique experiences or traumas. While each plan is client-specific, we pursue basic therapeutic aims with the model's techniques:

1. **We help children and adolescents achieve developmental tasks.** The first stage in Erikson's model involves **trust**. A child who has not had good bonding experiences as an infant may have difficulty trusting. Therefore, the treatment plan would, by necessity, work on this particular issue. For Violet, the client's having been deprived of any non-generic, mutually respectful I-Thou relationship is paramount. It may therefore take some time before the client will feel safe and trusting enough to engage in further therapeutic activities.

2. **We examine the client's contact skills** of looking, listening, tasting, touching, smelling, moving, talking. **If the youngster has difficulty making contact, we provide contact experiences through appropriate activities.**

3. **We look at resistance**—behavioral manifestations of the client's contact-boundary disturbances. These can be useful for self-protection and coping with the environment. But they can become the client's default processes, or way of being in the world, and generally cause difficulty.

    A. **We counter desensitization** by offering sensory experiences like finger painting, wet clay work, water play, sand touching, the orange exercise, music, discriminating sounds, tastes, smells—anything to open and enhance sensory awareness.

    B. **We discourage confluence:** The I-Thou relationship between therapist and client minimizes transference, which is a confluent (merged) state. Heightening differences and discovering—not just assuming—similarities; exploring the self with lists (Who Am I lists, What I Like, What I Don't Like); and setting clear limits all strengthen the self in the therapy process.

C. **We examine introjections:** Drawing or otherwise representing parts of the client's self they don't like, anger work, and self-nurturing work all allow clients to reveal and reintegrate hated aspects of their selves through understanding and compassion. Recognizing and loving these parts, rather than continuing to buy into faulty negative judgments of them imbibed in childhood, help clients replace self-critical "I should" and "I ought" with self-nurturing "I want."

D. **We disarm retroflection:** To act out clients' anger safely instead of letting it stay turned in against themselves, we have them experience "fighting" with batakas, "aggressive" games, puppets, contacting aggressive energy, body and breathing experiences, and other anger work.

E. **We utilize projection: Projective techniques** lead to owning the projections. These activities include the self-awareness game ("I'm aware of being hungry because my stomach hurts and is making noises"), making **"I statements"** instead of **"you statements,"** tuning into the body's intuitive sense within ("I want to go to bed now— true or false? False." "How did you know?" "I checked my body."), and other exercises in self-work.

Index

Introduction 3
Key Concepts and Definitions 4
    What is Gestalt Therapy with Children? 4
    The I-Thou Relationship 4
    Contact and Resistance 4
    Awareness and Experience 5
    The Senses and the Body 5
    Sense of Self 5
    Contact/Boundary Disturbances 6
    Self-Regulation 6
    Emotions 6
    Introjection, Confluence, Deflection, and Retroflection 6
    Self-Nurturing Work 7
    Polarities 7
    Unfinished Business 7

What Brings Children to Therapy? 8

First Session: Issues and Considerations 10
    Developmental Factors 11
    Confluence vs. Struggle for Self 11
    Egocentricity 11
    Introjects 11
    Getting Needs Met 11
    Expressing Emotions 11
    Limit-Setting 11
    Cultural Expectations 12
    Systems 12

The Therapeutic Process 12
    Establishing the Therapeutic Relationship 12
    Contact 12
    Contact Functions 12
    Self-Support 12
    Emotional Expression 13
    Self-Nurturing Work 13
    Dealing With Process 13

    Closing Session 13
    Family Work and Parent Education 13
    The Oaklander Model: Sequence of Work 16

Using Projective Techniques 18
    The Client's Therapeutic Steps 18

House Tree Person Drawing 20

Childhood Drawing 22

Safe Place Drawing 26

Rosebush Drawing 30

Table 1: Workshop 1 Metaphoric/Narrative Description Prompts and Responses 32

Emotions: Aggressive Energy and Anger 35
    Aggressive Energy 35
    The Many Faces of Anger 36
    Expressing Anger: Therapeutic Steps for Children and Adolescents 38
    Anger Drawing 40
    Anger Actions List: Expressing Anger Safely 42
    Clay Work: Something from Nothing Activity 44

Emotions: Grief and Loss 48
    Developmental Issues in Grief and Loss 49
    Grief at Each Developmental Stage: Reactions and Best Responses 50
    Grief Drawing 52

Guide to Brief Therapy with Children and Adolescents 54

Polarities 56
    Examples 57
    Suggested Activities Prompts 57

Puppets 58
    Suggested Activities Prompts 59

Table 2: Workshop 2 Metaphoric/Narrative Description Prompts and Responses 61

Picture Cards 62

Sand Tray Work 64

What to Observe and How to Respond: Levels of Sand Tray Work 65

Sand Tray Resources 67

Self-Acceptance and Self-Nurturing 68
Self-Nurturing Work 69
- Working with the Introjects 69
- The Self-Nurturing Process 69
- Giving Homework 70

Demon Drawing 72

Table 3: Workshop 3 Metaphoric/Narrative Description Prompts and Responses 75

Music Process 76

Termination: According to the Oaklander Model 80

Supplemental Activities 83
- Coat of Arms Drawing 84
- Coat of Arms Template 86
- Scribble Drawing 88
- Exercises to Strengthen the Self 90

References 92

Appendix 93
- Assessment 94
- Assessment Worksheet 98
- Treatment Plan 100

www.ingramcontent.com/pod-product-compliance
Lightning Source LLC
Chambersburg PA
CBHW080522030426
42337CB00023B/4599